Conversations with **Mies van der Rohe**

Conversations,
a Princeton Architectural Press series

Other books in this series

Ian McHarg
Conversations with Students
978-1-56898-620-3

Santiago Calatrava
Conversations with Students
978-1-56898-325-7

Le Corbusier
Talks with Students
978-1-56898-196-3

Louis I. Khan
Conversations with Students
978-1-56898-149-9

Rem Koolhaas
Conversations with Students
978-1-88523-202-1

Peter Smithson
Conversations with Students
978-1-56898-461-2

Conversations with Mies van der Rohe

Moisés Puente, editor

Princeton Architectural Press
37 East Seventh Street
New York, New York 10003

For a free catalog of books, call 1.800.722.6657
Visit our website at www.papress.com

First published under the title *Conversaciones
con Mies van der Rohe* by Editorial Gustavo Gili,
Barcelona, Spain, in 2006.
Epilogue © Iñaki Ábalos
Spanish edition © 2006 Editorial Gustavo Gili,
Barcelona
English edition © 2008 Princeton Architectural Press,
New York
Printed and bound in China
11 10 09 08 5 4 3 2 1 First edition

Text sources:
Mies van der Rohe. "Architecture and Technology."
Arts and Architecture 10 (1950).
"Interview with Mies van der Rohe." *Interbuild* 6
(1959).
"Peter Blake: A Conversation with Mies van der Rohe."
*Four Great Makers of Modern Architecture: Gropius,
Le Corbusier, Mies van der Rohe, Wright. The
Verbatim Record of a Symposium Held at the School
of Architecture, Columbia University, March–May,
1961.* New York: Da Capo Press, 1970.
"Conversations with Mies." In Peter, John. *The Oral
History of Modern Architecture: Interviews with the
Greatest Architects of the Twentieth Century.* New
York: Harry N. Abrams, 1994.

Cover photograph: © Werner Blaser

Graphic design: Marian Bardal
Translation of Iñaki Ábalos's text: Mark Gimson

Editing, English edition: Nicola Bednarek
Layout, English edition: Arnoud Verhaeghe

Special thanks to: Nettie Aljian, Sara Bader,
Dorothy Ball, Janet Behning, Becca Casbon,
Penny (Yuen Pik) Chu, Russell Fernandez,
Pete Fitzpatrick, Wendy Fuller, Jan Haux,
Clare Jacobson, Aileen Kwun, Nancy Eklund Later,
Linda Lee, Laurie Manfra, Katharine Myers,
Lauren Nelson Packard, Jennifer Thompson,
Paul Wagner, Joseph Weston, and Deb Wood of
Princeton Architectural Press
                                    —Kevin C. Lippert, publisher

Library of Congress Cataloging-in-Publication Data
Mies van der Rohe, Ludwig, 1886–1969.
  [Conversaciones con Mies van der Rohe. English]
  Conversations with Mies van der Rohe / Moisés
Puente, editor.
      p. cm. – (Conversations with students)
  Originally published: Conversaciones con Mies van
der Rohe. Barcelona, Spain : Editorial Gustavo Gili,
2006.
  ISBN 978-1-56898-753-8 (alk. paper)
  1. Mies van der Rohe, Ludwig, 1886–1969–
Interviews. 2. Architects–United States–Interviews.
3. Architecture–United States–20th century.
I. Puente, Moisés, 1969– II. Title.
NA1088.M65A35 2008
720.92–dc22

                                              2007037737

Contents

Architecture and Technology
1950

Technology is rooted in the past.
It dominates the present and tends into the future.
It is a real historical movement—
one of the great movements which shape and
represent their epoch.
It can be compared only with the Classic
discovery of man as a person,
the Roman will to power,
and the religious movement of the Middle Ages.
Technology is far more than a method,
it is a world in itself.
As a method it is superior in almost every respect.
But only where it is left to itself as in
the construction of machinery, or as in
gigantic structures of engineering, there
technology reveals its true nature.
There it is evident that it is not only a useful means,
that it is something, something in itself,
something that has a meaning and a powerful form—
so powerful in fact, that it is not easy to name it.
Is that still technology or is it architecture?
And that may be the reason why some people
are convinced that architecture will be outmoded
and replaced by technology.

Such a conviction is not based on clear thinking.
The opposite happens.
Wherever technology reaches its real fulfillment,
it transcends into architecture.
It is true that architecture depends on the facts,
but its real field of activity is the realm
of the significance.
I hope you will understand that architecture
has nothing to do with the inventions of forms.
It is not a playground for children, young or old.
Architecture is the real battleground of the spirit.
Architecture wrote the history of the epochs
and gave them their names.
Architecture depends on its time.
It is the crystallization of its inner structure,
the slow unfolding of its form.
That is the reason why technology and architecture
are so closely related.
Our real hope is that they grow together,
that someday the one be the expression of
the other.
Only then will we have an architecture worthy
of its name:
Architecture as a true symbol of our time.

Conversation One

860–880 Lake Shore Drive apartments (1948–51) and 900 Esplanade apartment, 1953–57, Chicago, Illinois © William S. Engdahl/Chicago Historical Society

What do you think about the technique of prefabrication?

I do not think it is an advantage to build planned packaged houses. If you prefabricate a house completely, it becomes an unnecessary restriction. The value of prefabrication is in the units and it is much better to have single elements prefabricated and to concentrate on the development of these elements. Thus the architect can use them in a free way. Otherwise architecture will be terribly boring.

In our last building on 860–880 Lake Shore Drive we had more than 3,000 individual windows but only two different window types. In 900 Esplanade we have, I would say, 10,000 windows all of the same type. That is enough prefabrication. But let me not be misunderstood. I think that an industrial process is not like a rubber stamp. Everything has to be put together and, as such, should have its own expression.

But would it not be better to have a standard system of components conforming to a standard dimension?

No. I do not think we need to give up our present freedom. Why should not each architect design his own standard? Otherwise you would have to tell everybody which standard they should use and that, I think, would be an impossible task. Some people, for instance, use 7-foot-high doors and have a plaster space over the top of the door. What I like to do is to make a door between floor and ceiling. So is my standard to be accepted or the other? I should mention here that we never use a ceiling that is lower than 8 feet. Ours are mostly 8.3 feet.

Has the mixed development concept of your Lafayette Park project particular significance as a new design approach by you?

We built the lower buildings for people who like to live on the ground. But others like to live up in the air. So here we built for

Previous spread: Mies van der Rohe at the Arts Club, Chicago, 1952

14

both. People used to say that high buildings were more costly than
low buildings but an interesting fact has come out of this Detroit
scheme. The apartments in the tall buildings are much cheaper
than the same apartments on the ground. Really much cheaper. So
I would not be surprised if, in such town development schemes, we
kill off the low house in the end.

But should people live high above the ground?
I think people should live as they like to live. Most people have
never lived in tall buildings. But others, and I know many, have lived
in them for years, and they are still fascinated with living there. But
if you build high, you must have enough space to live upon—as we
have in Detroit. There will be a huge 52-acre park in the center of
the buildings with trees and grass and no streets. Here we have
kept the streets out. All access is from perimeter roads which are
dead-ends.

Did the authorities ask you to plan this way?
No. We designed it our way from the start and once we were
satisfied the idea was a good one we made no concessions. We
had designed it, and we fully believed in it. We fought for it and we
even said that they must have it our way, otherwise we wouldn't
come to Detroit.

Can we always rejuvenate the middle of old cities?
No. Not always. But first, you can use up all the slums for new
development. In all the cities of the world there are large areas
of these. Also, you can avoid the spread of these silly suburban
houses. Chicago has thousands of them all over the place. Instead
of eating up the land they should have been developed as tall and

Right: Lafayette Park, Detroit, Michigan, 1955–63

low buildings in a reasonable way. And I don't say this is only work for architects. I think that developers could do it also. After all, most of these houses are made by developers and are made by builders. Very few are by architects.

But do they understand work such as yours?
Speaking for the Detroit project, I think we will have a great influence on new development. You will see. But generally, I think my work has so much influence because of its reasonableness. Everybody could do that. To do it well you don't have to have too much fantasy. You just need to use your brain. And, after all, that is something that everyone can do.

   Objective development is a question of education. Things become better and better by example. If there is no example, then people just talk. They talk about things they really don't know anything about, so they can't judge the difference between good or bad anyway.

Have you always felt this way?
No. I think it was a slow development. At the beginning everything was unclear and then the pattern and the answers gradually emerged. The more I searched for a deeper understanding of the problems, the clearer my work became. This development was from within myself. There were no influences in this process from outside.

What happened if you had a fine idea and couldn't get it built?
I can give you an example. I tried these glass skyscrapers first in 1922. That is, I designed them on paper and they worked fine. Then later, when we started our first skyscraper in Chicago,[1] we had

to build in concrete because it was just after World War II and we
could not get steel. Although I tried to find a solution in concrete,
at the same time I designed the same building in steel. I don't
know if you have ever seen this scheme[2] but after that we never
thought about concrete any more. From then on we built in steel.

Do you often design buildings without a client because you think a
site needs a particular building?
This is interesting because most of our designs are developed
long before there is a practical possibility of carrying them out.
I do that on purpose and have done it all my life. I do it when I
am interested in something. I do it just to hope that one day the
building will be lived in and liked.

You visualize a scheme when you see an empty site?
Well, not for every site. But for some, yes. Take Chicago, for
example. I perhaps think in my mind that there should be a large
hall for conventions. All right, then we start to design and try the
idea out. This is often with no motive but to experiment.

Do you try to influence people to get it built?
Sometimes it happens that they see the scheme somewhere and
they come to us to do the work.

Would you comment on architect/client relationship?
Never talk to a client about architecture. Talk to him about his
children. That is simply good politics. He will not understand what
you have to say about architecture most of the time. An architect
of ability should be able to tell a client what he wants. Most of the
time a client never knows what he wants. He may, of course, have

Following pages: Convention Hall (preliminary scheme), Chicago, 1953

some very curious ideas, and I do not mean to say that they are silly ideas. But being untrained in architecture they just cannot know what is possible and what is not possible.

But perhaps he would not like the finished building?
That would not matter at all, although I have never had this experience. I may have had many wrangles with clients while a building was being designed, and often while it is being built, but always, in the end, they have been satisfied with the way I did it.

Do you submit alternative schemes to a client?
No. Only one. Always. And the best one that we can give. That is where you can fight for what you believe in. He doesn't have to choose. How can he choose? He hasn't the capacity to choose. No, it is much better to have just one idea, and if the idea is clear, then you can fight for it. That is how you can get things done.

Has any one year particular significance in the development of the modern world?
I would say that 1926 was the most significant year. Looking back it seems that it was not a year in the sense of time. It was a year of great realization of awareness. It seems to me that at certain times in the history of man the understanding of certain situations ripens. Putting it another way, it seems that a particular situation will be ripe at a certain time and will be understood. That is why great people who may never know each other can talk, simultaneously, about the same things.

21

Could 1959 be a similar ripening period?

I think there is a lot we do not understand about the mental
processes but, if the situation is strong enough, people will
become sensitive to the situation and will then work on it. I think
that is how it happens but I am not sure if it is happening today.

Can this awareness be forced?

I do not think so. I think it lies in the nature of things. It takes time.
It took me a long time to understand the relationship between
ideas and between objective facts. But after I clearly understood
this relationship, I didn't fool around with other wild ideas. That
is one of the main reasons why I just make my scheme as simple
as possible. I have always worked for ordered relationships. Take
the buildings on the Illinois Institute of Technology (IIT) campus,
for example. There we drew a net of 24 feet by 24 feet all over
the campus so at all the crossings we could put columns. It is
thus possible to connect individual buildings at any point and still
preserve the original system.

But your awareness was a long realization process?

At the beginning it was more of an instinctive drive. Later on it
became more and more a conscious awareness. But, again, all this
was from within me. Always. In my interview with the BBC[3] I talked
of the three other people in Europe who, although I didn't know
them, were thinking in 1926 what I was thinking. Their business
was to get this thing clear in their minds and to write their books
about it. In the same way I had to build, and I was very happy with
the results.

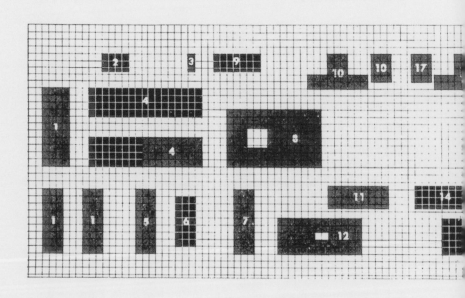

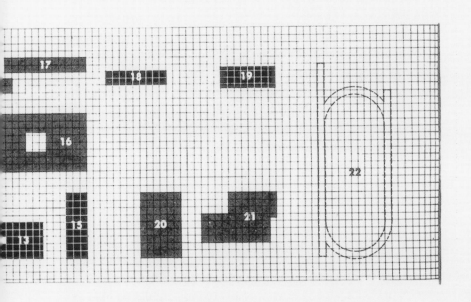

Illinois Institute of Technology (IIT), campus master plan, Chicago, 1939–40

Can architects work together on major projects?

I do not think very much of this sort of forced teamwork myself. The teamwork in our field is between architect, mechanical engineer, and structural engineer. That is where teamwork comes in. It is no use working with other architects. What can they do? Who does what? I think it would be better, say, to have different designs and choose. After all, why should I discuss my ideas with someone else? The most important things cannot be discussed anyway. I would prefer not to work with other people. I work with larger firms of architects in different ways but I don't discuss my ideas with them. I would never do that.

The same with the structural engineer. We tell him what we want and he tells us if it is possible. In the field of design the structural engineers, with a few exceptions like Pier Luigi Nervi, do not know what they are doing.

Can one man have a clear idea of right and wrong? Or is this conceit?

I am with the single man. When an idea is good—and it is a clear idea—then it should only come from one man. If the idea is demonstrated in an objective way, everybody should be able to understand it. But, of course, few people ever do.

Have we moved into a new era of thought, do you think?

I think there is no more difference in the arrival of nuclear fission than there was in the arrival of the aeroplane. People do not, I think, change basically. We can easily become too influenced by what we read in the newspapers. I think this so-called Space Age is just a technological problem of the universe.

25

Its existence has no bearing on mankind?

No. I don't think so. It certainly has no bearing on the spiritual development. But it does have a strong bearing on the actual facts of life as, for example, the fact that maybe in a short time this atomic energy will be much cheaper and of greater use to everybody. I hope so.

In splitting the atom could we not be near to comprehension of the life force?

Between the ideas and the objective facts I think the problems are always the same. Whatever the objective facts are, these problems will never change. There is a true relationship between these things, and it is understanding this relationship that is the challenge to human beings. To become aware of this is a question of deep insight and education.

Many things in life should then be experienced?

Certainly. These inventions and industrial and scientific discoveries belong to the objective facts, but they have nothing to do with the relationship of the ideas to the facts. The ideas must be understood if we are to understand life.

But ideas must come first to change facts?

No. The facts are given to us. We have had them for hundreds of years. When, in the sixteenth and seventeenth centuries, the first modern scientists were experimenting, they had no idea what would come out of their ideas. They had no influence on the use man would make of them. Now we have science, we have technology, and we have industrialization. All are accepted as a part of progressive existence. The question is what to do with them. That is the human side of this problem.

We must cope then with what we have created?
We have to know that life cannot be changed by us. It will be changed. But not by us. We can only guide the things that can cause physical change. But I would criticize, for example, a nuclear scientist who discovers a natural phenomenon but does not appreciate the consequences of his discovery. Yes, I would criticize him for that. It would be better if he could see. But maybe he can't. After all, he has to do with facts and not with ideas. It is for all men, not just a few, to use all these things for the best for all of us. That, I think, is what we should do with our lives.

London, 1959

1. Mies van der Rohe is referring to the 860–880 Lake Shore Drive apartments, Chicago, Illinois, USA, 1948–51.
2. 900 Esplanade apartment buildings, Chicago, Illinois, USA, 1953–57.
3. In a 1959 interview with Graeme Shankland for the BBC, Mies talked about the year 1926 and mentioned Max Scheler, Rudolf Schwarz, and Alfred North Whitehead and their works: "Max Scheler wrote his book on the forms of knowledge and society.... In this year Rudolph Schwarz wrote his book on technology.... And in the same year, in 1926, Whitehead started his talks which he later published." Max Scheler, *Die Wissenformen und die Gesellschaft* (Leipzig: Der neue-Geist Verlag, 1926); Rudolf Schwarz, *Wegweisung der Technik* (Potsdam: Müller & Kiepenheuer, 1926); [also included in: *Wegweisung der Technik und andere Schriften zum neuen Bauen, 1926–1961* (Braunschweig/Wiesbaden: Vieweg, 1979)] and Alfred North Whitehead, *Science and the Modern World* (Cambridge: The University Press, 1926).

Conversation Two

What is the role of structure in architecture?
During all my life I was thinking about architecture: all the time, what it is and how it could be done in our time. I think that a clear structure is a great help for architecture. I am old now, you know, and I cannot do anything that is not clearly conceived.

To me, structure is something like logic. It is the best way to do things and to express them. I am very skeptical about emotional expressions. I don't trust them, and I don't think they will last for long.

Do you feel that you have come to your kind of architecture through construction and through knowing about how things are built, rather than through theory?

I think that goes together. I thought about architecture, and then I tried architecture to prove it. Often experience showed that my thoughts were in no way right, but many times experience proved my thoughts correct.

What have you learned from the old things in Europe? A lot of people, when describing your work, refer to Karl Friedrich Schinkel and even to the Renaissance.

When I came as a young man to Berlin[1] and looked around, I was interested in Schinkel because Schinkel was the most important architect in Berlin. There were several others, but Schinkel was the most important man. His buildings were an excellent example of Classicism—the best I know. And certainly I became interested in that. I studied him carefully and came under his influence. That could have happened to anybody. I think Schinkel had wonderful constructions, excellent proportions, and good detailing.

What about the way Schinkel places his buildings on pedestals?
I think that is a good way of doing it, in spite of the fact that it is a
classic way of doing it.

In your early work there was a tremendously sudden break.
Whereas you had been working in the classical tradition up to
the beginning of World War I, in 1919 you seem to have broken
completely with everything you had done before.
I think the break started long before. The break started when I
was in the Netherlands working on the problem of the Kröller-
Müller Museum. There I saw and studied carefully Hendrik Petrus

Berlage. I read his books and his theme that architecture should be construction, clear construction. His architecture was brick, and it may have looked medieval, but it was always clear.

You know, people who refer to your work now as being classical in spirit also say that the tradition of architecture in America, at least in the past one hundred years, has been romantic and anti-Classical; organic in the case of Frank Lloyd Wright and quite romantic in the case of Henry H. Richardson. Do you feel that your architecture is in any way in conflict with the basic motives of American architecture—that it is a stationary kind of thing as

Above: Full-scale model of the Kröller-Müller Museum (project), Wassenaar, The Netherlands, 1912

opposed to a moving kind of thing, which seems to be the American theme?

I never think about it in these terms. And I think it is quite dangerous. You know, we had in Europe and in England William Morris, some arts and crafts people, and we had them in Germany. We were quite romantic. I think that the main difference is that in the nineteenth century there was a great confusion. You could say that is a phase of democracy, but democracy does not have to be confused.

If you compare the Barcelona Pavilion with the first building at IIT,[2] the Barcelona Pavilion had a very strong sweep. It was almost a building in motion, at least that is the way it looks in photographs. The buildings at IIT are very stable, very clear. They are objects that are standing there and are completely enclosed within themselves. Don't you feel there is quite a change between those two buildings?

No. If you remember, I made one design for the campus (it was not built) where I removed most of the streets, so that I could place the buildings freely there. I was told by Henry Heald, the president, that it could not be done at the moment. They would not permit me until much later to remove the streets. So I was confronted with the past—I had to develop a plan in the normal block pattern, and I did that. You cannot do much about it. And there is another question, too. To make things in motion, is that not a handicap to modern architecture and to building? We had to build school buildings, and we didn't often know for what they would be used. So we had to find a system that made it possible to use these buildings as classrooms, as workshops, or as laboratories.

One of the things that is sometimes suggested about your idea of a universal space, a building that might be used for one thing today and something entirely different ten or twenty years from now, is that the American economy depends upon rapid obsolescence of buildings, so that people can be kept at work. Do you think that the idea of a universal kind of architecture is a threat to the idea of some kind of accelerated obsolescence?

First, let me say that I think that the idea of rapid obsolescence is a very funny idea. I don't even think it is a good idea. I think that obsolescence is a kind of excuse. I don't think it is a real fact. There are things that don't have to last for a lifetime. This suit, for instance. In older times, we had one suit when we married, and we kept that all the time for good. Otherwise, we had only working clothes. That is no longer necessary—that it will last forever. There are things that can be replaced and of necessity will be replaced, but I wonder if the buildings will be replaced.... No, I think we should be reasonable. You don't have to build like the pyramids, to last thousands of years. But a building should live as long as it can live. There is no reason to make it just provisional. In that case, they should build a tent!

I come more and more to the conviction that architecture has a certain relation to civilization. If somebody says architecture is not related to civilization, there isn't any use talking about it. I personally believe that it does, and this seems to me the main task we have: to build an architecture which expresses this kind of civilization we are in. That is the only way I can see to over-come chaos.

Our civilization depends largely on science and technology. That is a fact. Everybody should see that. The question is how far we can express that. You know, we architects are in this peculiar position. We should express the time and yet build in it. But in the end, I really believe that architecture can only be the expression of its civilization.

What would you say is the main problem of architecture in America? What can architecture do to change the American scene as it looks now, and how should architects go about it?

Yes, I think that is in fact the most important question. You know, if somebody doesn't agree with me that there is a relation, that architecture is only possible in relation to civilization, then there is no use in talking about it. But if somebody accepts that, then we can ask ourselves: what kind of relation is there, and what is our civilization like? Everybody talks about it, but it is really difficult to define. Civilization is a process partly of the past and partly of the present, and it is partly open to the future. So it is really difficult to find—in this moving process—the characteristic of civilization.

It is not enough that somebody has some ideas. It is not enough to just say these things *are* architecture or just say, "That is what I like to do." We had that when I was young. I listened to these great people, around 1900. We were talented, we had everything you could ask for to work in the field of architecture, but we were just subjective, in my opinion, as most people are subjective today. I think we can move on only if we really find some ground to stand on. Architecture, in my opinion, is not a subjective affair. The tendency should be in an objective direction.

To a great many artists (including some architects) the natural reaction to our time is to revolt and be different. Do you think that it is excusable for an architect to react to his time by being different from his time?

No, I think it isn't. I believe he cannot, so that makes it hopeless
to try. But I don't believe that everything has to be the same.
But there must be, and I am sure there are, certain fundamental
principles that are given. We are, to a very small degree, craftsmen.
We build these machines. We use them. More and more buildings
become the product of machine production.

In the last few years Le Corbusier has been going in the opposite
direction—making buildings more crude. There are almost no
details in his buildings any more. They are crudely done and
deliberately so. Do you think that that is the wrong direction to
take today?

I would not say the wrong direction. Le Corbusier, when he made
his postwar buildings, had to work with those primitive craftsmen,
and I think that is one of the reasons why he could make them
primitive. It was in France outside of Marseilles.[3] What would you
think of such a rough building on Park Avenue? Where the people
that go into the building and out of the building are well-dressed?

If you were building in India, as Le Corbusier is today, how do you
think you would build?

As simply as possible. If I could not use advanced technological
means, then I would have to do what they did in former times—
work with the hands.

If we are going to have these very complex mechanical systems
in buildings, doesn't it make some sort of sense to dramatize the
mechanics of a building?

I think structural elements are very essential elements, and I
think that pipes are not. The structure can be integrated into

architecture, but I don't think that pipes can. We can bring the pipes into our buildings, where they belong, you know.

Le Corbusier, in some of his buildings, has dramatized the mechanical parts, so maybe there are ways of elevating pipes into architecture, too.

This is possible, and I think that Le Corbusier did it well. But not everybody can do that, and I see no reason why everybody should do that.

When you talk about structure, I think that most of the time you still talk about rectangular structures because they are the most reasonable, practical, and economical. But now that it is at least possible to have a very fluid structure, what do you think might happen to architecture if those very fluid structures take over from the simple rectangle?

I don't think that they will take over. I think fluid structures, like shells, have a very limited use. They are, in fact, open structures. You build a one-story building, and you can do what you like with it; maybe in a two-, even three-story building, you are to a certain degree free. But then it ends. How can you use them in a tall building? For most things we do we need space: a living space, a working place. If there is no reason for it, why make them fluid? A rectangular space is a good space, maybe much better than a fluid space. If you have some particular function or something that is fluid inside, I think it is a good idea to make it curved. But it is not a good idea to make an office space with organic form just for aesthetic reasons. You can do it if you have a theater, or a single building, or a site where you can be free-moving. But most of our buildings are quite patterned by the city.

People who are very much interested in these fluid structures think that if you were to do a whole city, it would be a rather dull place—that the buildings would be very much alike, and that maybe there is some need for variation here and there.

But take the medieval cities—that is a good example. All the houses are really the same. All plans are really the same. But who could afford it put in a fine entrance hall; you might buy and put on a fine door knocker; and if somebody could afford a bay window, he did that. But the plans are the same, and how rich is the medieval city!

Wright's buildings in the cities, at least his buildings in the last twenty years, seemed to have been very antagonistic towards the city.

Yes, certainly. I do not share his position, you know. I believe that you have to accept the reality. I don't think anybody can change it by a theoretical formula. I have seen that tried too often, and it has gone to pieces. I would accept it and then do something with it. That is the problem, you know. People often think I have a formula when I talk about structure. They think that I am talking about a steel beam. I'm not, you know. That has nothing to do with it. You can build in concrete. But if I had to build in concrete, I would not build like Wright. I see no reason for that, because I believe that these Wright things don't belong to our time.

Do you think that in a free enterprise democracy, where everyone is free to do just about what he wants within very slight limitations, that it is possible to create architectural order?

Yes, I think it would be an order in freedom.

But do you think that it requires, perhaps, discipline on the part
of the architects before it could work? Or how would you put it?
**I certainly think that it requires discipline on the part of the archi-
tects. I think even Wright needed a lot of discipline in his work.**

It seems to me that in some of your early buildings like the
Barcelona Pavilion, there are traces of Wright's principles. To
what extent has Wright impressed you and influenced your work?
**For Philip Johnson's book,[4] I wrote about Wright and the influence
he had on us in Europe. Certainly, I was very much impressed
by the Robie House and by the office building in Buffalo.[5] Who
wouldn't be impressed? He was certainly a great genius—there
is no question about that. You know, it is very difficult to go in his**

Minerals and Metals Research Building, Illinois Institute of Technology (IIT), 1943
© Hedrich-Blessing/Chicago Historical Society

direction. You sense that his architecture is based on fantasy. You have to have fantasy in order to go in this direction, and if you have fantasy, you don't go in his direction, you go in your own. Wright had a great influence, but very late in his life. But his influence on the face of America is quite modest.

A lot of art critics claim that your work is very much influenced by De Stijl, by Theo van Doesburg.
No, that is absolute nonsense, you know.

Why don't you explain why?
Van Doesburg saw these drawings of the office building. I explained it to him, and I said, "This is skin-and-bones architecture." After that he called me an anatomical architect. I liked van Doesburg, but it was not as though he knew very much about architecture. He designed houses or buildings together with Cor van Eesteren, the city planner. But mostly he was interested in his particular kind of art. Like Piet Mondrian. Once in Düsseldorf he proposed the dictum that everything should be square. But there is no influence. The same people claim that I was influenced by Mondrian in the first building for the IIT campus, the Minerals and Metals Research Building. This one has a wall that they say looks like Mondrian. But I remember very well how it came about. Everything was donated for this whole building: the site—we had 64 feet from the railroad to the sidewalk; somebody gave them a traveling crane—it was 40 feet wide, so we needed 42 feet from center of column to center of column. The rest was laboratories, you know. Everything was there—we needed steel bracing in the wall, the brick wall. It was a question of the building code. You can only make an 8-inch wall so big, otherwise you have to reinforce

it. So we did that. Then, when everything was finished, the people from the Minerals and Metals Research Building, the engineers, they came and said, "We need here a door." So I put in a door. And the result was the Mondrian!

What about the constructivists—the Russian constructivists? Were you interested in their work?

No, I was never interested in formalistic ideas. I was very strongly opposed even to Kazimir Malevich, you know. Very constructivistic. I was interested in construction, but not in play with forms.

One of the things that is interesting about you, at least to those of us who know you today, is that you seem rather conservative in many ways—in your bearing, in your work, in your preferences, and so on, and yet in the early twenties and right after World War I you must have been a wild radical. You were involved in very radical movements at the time. How do you account for the change?

I don't think there is a change. I think there is a natural development. In the early twenties I tried to understand architecture, and I tried to find positive solutions, and I am still doing that now, you know. I don't construct sociological systems. But I am very much interested in the question of civilization. What is it? What is going on? This is not the system or the work of one man. It is the work of many. Civilization is given to us from the past, and all we can do is to guide it. I don't think we can change it fundamentally. We can do something with it in a good way or in a bad way.

Mies van der Rohe with his fourth-year students at the IIT, 1939 © IIT Archives, Chicago

IIT, which is the expression of your ideas on education, is perhaps the most rigid and formal school in America today. What motivated you to make IIT what it is, and what do you expect the students to get out of the school?

You know, when I came here to the school[6] and I had to change the curriculum, I was thinking to find a method which teaches the student how to make a good building. Nothing else. First, we taught them how to draw. The first year is spent on that. And they learn how to draw. Then we taught them construction in stone, in brick, in wood, and make them learn something about engineering. We talked about concrete and steel. Then we taught them something about functions of buildings, and in the junior year we tried to teach them a sense of proportion and a sense of space. And only in the last year we came to a group of buildings. And there I see no rigidness in the curriculum at all. Because we try to make them aware of the problems involved. We don't teach them solutions, we teach them a way to solve problems.

You read a great deal of philosophy. What philosophers interest you most...and what historians?

I was interested in architecture all my life. And I have tried to find out what was said about architecture. I have tried to find out what can influence architecture. I feel that architecture belongs to certain epochs; it expresses the real essence of its times. It was to us a question of truth. How can we find out, know, and feel what is the truth?

What I say is the result of a lifetime of work. It is not a special idea I have when I say that architecture should be the expression of structure. But the interrelation of these things was not clear at the time. So all my reading was about what influences architecture.

When I read about sociology, I wanted to know what ideas would be an influence really on our time.

I didn't want to change the time; I wanted to express the time. That was my whole project. I didn't want to change anything. I really believe that all these ideas, the sociological ideas and even the technological ideas, would have an influence on architecture. But they are not architecture themselves. What we really need is to know how to build with any material, and that is what is missing today.

Chicago, 1960

1. Mies moved to Berlin in 1905, where he worked in Bruno Paul's studio.
2. The first work built by Mies in America was the Minerals and Metals Research Building on the IIT campus, Chicago, Illinois, USA, 1942–43.
3. Le Corbusier, Unité d'Habitation, Marseilles, France, 1946–52.
4. Mies wrote an article titled "Frank Lloyd Wright" for the (never published) catalog of Wright's exhibition at the Museum of Modern Art in New York in 1940, a text that Johnson included in his book on Mies, *Mies van der Rohe* (New York: The Museum of Modern Art, 1947), 195–96. In this article Mies said: "At this moment, so critical for us [1910], the exhibition of the work of Frank Lloyd Wright came to Berlin....The encounter was destined to prove of great significance to the European development."
5. Frank Lloyd Wright, Robie House, Chicago, Illinois, USA, 1908; Larkin Co. office building, Buffalo, New York, USA, 1904 (demolished in 1950).
6. Mies was dean of the IIT School of Architecture from 1938 to 1958.

Conversation Three

Previous page: Mies van der Rohe in his Chicago apartment, 1965

This text is the result of two edited conversations, taking place in 1955 and 1964.

1964 What first interested you in architecture?

I learned from my father. He was a stonemason. He liked to do good work. I remember in my hometown in Aachen was the cathedral. This octagon was built by Charlemagne. In different centuries they did something different with it. Sometime in the Baroque they plastered the whole thing and made ornaments in it. When I was young they took the plaster out. Then they didn't have the money to go further, so you saw the real stones. When I looked at the old building that had nothing on it, just fine brickwork or stonework—a building that was really clear and with really good craftsmanship—I would have given all the other things for one of these buildings. Later they covered it with marble again, but I must say it was much more impressive without the marble.

Tell me, were you influenced in your thinking by things other than architecture—music or painting?

Yes, I may have been later. But not when I was young. I didn't have any particular relation to other arts.

Did reading have anything to do with your thinking?

Yes, quite a lot. I left school when I was fourteen years old, so I had no education. I worked for an architect. When I came to his office, he said, "Here is your table." I cleaned it up and looked in the drawer. What I found there were two things, a magazine called *Die Zukunft*. It was a weekly magazine. It was a very interesting magazine. It was partly a political magazine, but in the way as Walter Lippmann would talk about politics, not a party affair. It was a cultural magazine, let us say that. It talked about music. It talked about poetry. It talked about architecture, but very seldom. That was one thing.

Then I found another pamphlet about the Pierre-Simon Laplace theory. That was these two things. From then on I started to read this magazine, *Die Zukunft*. I bought it every Sunday morning and read it. Then I started to read.

A few years later, when I came to Berlin, I had to build a house for a philosopher.[1] It was at the university in Berlin. There I met quite a number of people, and I started to read more and more. When this philosopher came to my office for the first time—I had an office in my apartment, and my books were lying on a huge drafting board, about a foot high—he looked around and he saw all these books. He said, "For heaven's sake, who advised you on your library?" I said, "Nobody. I started to buy books and read them." He was very surprised. He saw no discipline in it or anything like that.

At that time, we were working for Peter Behrens.[2] There were other architects in Berlin. Alfred Messel, he was a very fine architect, but a Palladio man or something like that.

I was interested in what architecture is. I asked somebody, "What is architecture?" But he didn't answer me. He said, "Just forget it. Just work. You will find that out by yourself later." I said, "That's a fine answer to my question." But I wanted to know more. I wanted to find out. That was the reason I read; for nothing else. I wanted to find out things, I wanted to be clear. What is going on. What is our time and what is it all about. Otherwise, I didn't think we would be able to do something reasonable. In this way, I read a lot. I bought all these books and paid for them. I read them in all the fields.

53

Do you still read?
Yes, I do. And I read very often the old books. The New York
Chapter of the American Institute of Architects (AIA) once had
some affair going on. I said, "When I left Germany, I had about
three thousand books. I made a list, and they shipped me three
hundred." I said, "I could send back two hundred and seventy.
Thirty is all I wanted to have."

I was interested in the philosophy of values and problems of
the spirit. I was also very much interested in astronomy and natural sciences. I asked myself the question, "What is the truth? What
is the truth?" until I stopped at Thomas Aquinas. I found the
answer there.

So, for other things, what is order? Everybody talks about it
but nobody could tell you what it is. Until I read Augustine about
sociology. There was a mess as great as in architecture then.
You could read a lot of sociological books and you were not
wiser than before.

Do you feel that the thinking of people who sought truth in other
periods is applicable today?
Oh, certainly, I am sure. There are certain truths; they don't wear
out. I am quite sure of that. I cannot talk for other people. I just
followed what I needed. I want this clarity. I could have read other
books, a lot of poetry or others. But I didn't. I read these books
where I could find the truth about certain things.

Did your father or mother influence you in thinking this way?
Not at all. No. My father said, "Don't read these dumb books.
Work." He was a craftsman.

Were there great works or great masters who influenced your own thinking about architecture?

Yes, there is no question. I think if somebody takes his work seriously and even if he is relatively young, he will be influenced by other people. You just cannot help that. It is a fact.

First of all, I was influenced by old buildings. I looked at them, people built them. I don't know the names, and I don't know what it was—mostly very simple buildings. When I was really young, not even twenty years old, I was impressed by the strength of these old buildings because they didn't even belong to any epoch. But they were there for one thousand years and still there and still impressive, and nothing could change it. And all the styles, the great styles, passed, but they were still there. They didn't lose anything. They were ignored through certain architectural epochs, but they were still there and still as good as they were on the first day they were built.

Then I worked with Peter Behrens. He had a great sense of the great form. That was his main interest; and that I certainly understood and learned from him.

By great form what do you mean?

Oh, let us say like the Palazzo Pitti. It is something, the monumental form. Let me put it this way: I was lucky enough when I came to the Netherlands to be confronted with Hendrik Petrus Berlage's work. There was construction. What made the strongest impression on me was the use of brick and so on, the honesty of materials and so on. I never forget the lesson I got there just by looking at his buildings. I had only a few talks with Berlage, but not about that. We never talked about architecture together.

Do you think he knew that you sensed what he was doing?

No, I don't think so. I cannot see any reason why he should have because we didn't talk about it. I was really a young boy then. But I really learned this idea from him. I must have been open for this particular view because of the old buildings I had seen.

And I learned a lot from Frank Lloyd Wright. I would say that. I think more as a liberation. I felt much freer by seeing what he did. The way he puts a building in the landscape and the free way he uses space and so on.

Then those were the influences in your approach to architecture?

But my architectural philosophy came out of reading philosophical books. I cannot tell you at the moment where I read it, but I know I read it somewhere, that architecture belongs to the epoch and not even to the time, to a real epoch.

Since I understood that, I would not be for fashion in architecture. I would look for more profound principles. And since I know by reading and studying books that we are under the influence of science and technology, I would ask myself, "What can that be? What result comes from this fact? Can we change it, or can we not change it?" And the answer to this question gave me the direction which I followed, not what I liked. I often throw things out I like very much. They are dear to my heart, but when I have a better conviction, a better idea, a clearer idea, then I follow the clearer idea. And after a while I found the Washington Bridge most beautiful, the best building in New York. Maybe at the beginning I wouldn't. That grew. But first I had to conquer the idea and later I appreciated it as beauty.

56

So you sought what was characteristic of the epoch.

What is the essence of the epoch. And that is the only thing we really can express, and that is worth to express.

There is another thing that just comes to my mind. Thomas Aquinas says, "Reason is the first principle of all human work." Now when you have grasped that once, then you act accordingly. So I would throw everything out that is not reasonable.

I don't want to be interesting. I want to be good.

You often find in books that have nothing to do with architecture the very important things. Erwin Schrödinger, the physicist, talks about general principles, and he said the creative vigor of a general principle depends precisely on its generality. That is exactly what I think about when I talk about structure in architecture. It is not a special solution. It is the general idea.

Sometimes people say, "How do you feel if somebody copies you?" I say that is not a problem for me. I think that is the reason we are working, that we find something everybody can use. We hope only that he uses it right.

In other words, copies are an affirmation that you have found a general solution.

Yes, that is what I call the common language, too. That is what I'm working on. I am not working on architecture, I am working on architecture as a language, and I think you have to have a grammar in order to have a language. It has to be a living language, but still you come in the end to the grammar. It is a discipline. And then you can use it for normal purposes and you speak in prose. And if you are good at that, you speak a wonderful prose, and if you are really good, you can be a poet. But it is the same language, that is the characteristic. A poet doesn't produce a different language for each poem. That's not necessary; he uses the same language, he uses even the same words. In music it is always the same and the same instruments, most of the time. I think it is the same in architecture.

If you have to construct something you can make a garage out of it or you can make a cathedral out of it. We use the same means, the same structural methods for all these things. It has nothing to do with the level you are working on. What I am driving at is to develop a common language, not particularly individual ideas. I think that is the biggest point in our whole time. We have no real common language. To build that, if possible, if we can do that, then we can build what we like and everything is all right. I see no reason why that should not be the case. I am quite convinced that will be the task for the future.

I think there will be certain influences, climatic influences, but that will only color what is done. I think a much greater influence is the influence of science and technology that is worldwide and that will take all these old cultures away and everybody will do the same. Just this light coloration.

In other words, you feel we are in a period where there can be an architectural vocabulary?

Oh, certainly, there's no question about that. I think that this is a human desire to do something reasonable. I see no difference if there is something reasonable in California, in the Mediterranean, or in Norway. They should do it with reason. If they would work with reason and would not have fancy ideas, particularly architectural ideas, everything would be much better.

58

You would say that the people recognize a reasonable and
honest approach?

Certainly. Let us take an example—the mechanic in a garage
today. He is very much interested in all the technological means
we have. He takes all that for granted. You have no personal ideas
about these things. When he sticks to that, then he is on the
common plane.

Do you mind working with engineers?

No, just the opposite, I love it if I get a good one. There are
things that cannot be done without engineers. You cannot know
everything. I think architects should understand more about
engineering and the engineers should know a little more about
architecture.

Will new materials greatly change the style of our times?

No, I don't think so, because what I tried to do in architecture is to
develop a clear structure. We are just confronted with the material.
How to use it in the right way is what you have to find out. It has
nothing to do with the shape. What I do—what you call my kind of
architecture—we should just call it a structural approach. We don't
think about the form when we start. We think about the right way to
use the materials. Then we accept the result.

Grand ideas we keep high in the air when we are working.
We don't want them to come down. Often we are ourselves
surprised what comes out of it. I collect the facts—all the facts,
as much as I can get. I study these facts, and then I act
accordingly.

Maybe one of the problems of Frank Lloyd Wright's style is that it is
not a vocabulary in that sense.
It is not that. It is much too individualistic to be that. We know he's
a genius. There is no question about that. But I think he cannot
have real followers. In order to do things as he does it, you need a
lot of fantasy and, if you have fantasy, you will do it differently. I am
quite sure it is an individualistic approach, and I don't go this way. I
go a different way. I am trying to go an objective way.

Have there been architects of the past who have developed a style
that lasted as a vocabulary?
Andrea Palladio, certainly. It lasted. It is still among us in certain
cases. Even though his forms have changed, his spirit is still there
in many cases.

Do you think there is a desire on the part of people for natural
materials that are in a sense rich? For instance, I've always felt
disappointed that the Resor House was never built.
Yes, I was sorry, too. I think it is a very good building.

Do you think these rich materials tend to give a humanity to it?
It is not necessary, but it can be rich. But it is not necessary. It
could very well be simple. It would not change that.

You mean the Resor House wouldn't have had to be built with
teak?
No, it was not necessary at all. It could have been in any other kind
of wood and still be a good building. It would not be as fine as teak.
    In fact, I think that the Barcelona Pavilion, if I would have built it
in brick, it would be as good a building. I am quite sure it would not

have been as successful as marble, but that has nothing to do
with the idea.

What do you think of the use of color in architecture?
In our IIT campus I painted the steel black. At the Farnsworth
House I painted it white because it was in the green. It was in
the open. I could use any color.

And you've even been known to chrome it as you did in the
Barcelona Pavilion.
Oh, certainly, yes. I would do that. I love natural materials or
metallic things. I very seldom have used colored walls, for instance.
I would really like to give it to Pablo Picasso or to Paul Klee. In fact,
I ordered from Klee a large picture—two pictures—one side white
and the other black. I said, "I don't care what you paint on it."

So if it were a problem of color you would give it to a master.
Oh, certainly, yes. I would do that.

Above: Resor House, Jackson Hole, Wyoming, 1937–39.
Collage with a reproduction of Paul Klee's *Colorful Meal* (1939).

1964 If I were subjective, I would be a painter, not an architect. There I can express anything I like, but in buildings I have to do what has to be done. Not that I like it particularly; just what's best to be done. I often throw out ideas I was in love with, but when I thought them through I just had to throw them out. That is the difference. It is not so much the function. You cannot be really subjective. It looks funny in buildings. You have to be good, a stonemason or a timber man. There is nothing funny about that. In painting you can express the slightest emotion, but with a beam of wood or a piece of stone you cannot do much about it. If you try to do much about it, then you lose the character of your material. I think architecture is an objective art.

What was the Bauhaus? Why did you associate your own name and talents with it?

I think Walter Gropius could answer this question best because he was the founder and to me that is the Bauhaus. He left the Bauhaus and gave it into the hands of Hannes Meyer. At this time it became more a political instrument or was used not so much by Hannes Meyer but by younger people. Hannes Meyer, in my opinion, was not a strong man. He was taken in by these young people. I can understand that, too. But there was a certain difference. You could say that was the second phase of the Bauhaus, quite different from Gropius's phase. The Bauhaus from 1919 to 1932 was in no way one affair. It was quite different.

I came to the Bauhaus when the Bauhaus had trouble for political reasons. The city, which was Democratic or Social Democratic, had to pay for it. They said we will not do that anymore. Gropius and the mayor of Dessau came to me. They explained that to me and asked me to take it over.[3] They thought

Mies van der Rohe with his students at the Bauhaus, Dessau, Germany

if I would not do it, it would be closed. I went there and made it clear to the students, as clear as I could, "You have to work here and I can assure you who doesn't work I will throw out. I have nothing against any political idea that is here." I spent my time to teach them something, and they had to work on it. But I was not as involved as Gropius was. That was his idea. We were working in the same direction.

At Gropius's seventieth birthday I talked about the Bauhaus.[4] I said that I didn't believe that it was the propaganda which made it known all over the world, but that it was a new idea. Propaganda would never be so strong as to do this work. But I think Gropius can tell you more about it than I can.

Would there have been a Bauhaus if there had been no Gropius?
No, I think there would not have been a Bauhaus. There would have been another school. The school was there when it was in Weimar. If I'm not mistaken, I think that Gropius was proposed by van de Velde, who was the head of the school in Weimar. When he left Weimar he proposed Gropius as his successor.

Getting the different people was Gropius's doing. There is no doubt about that. He brought these people. He must have seen that these people were driving in a different direction, too. But that they were good people, that was Gropius's doing.

How important to the Bauhaus was the climate of the Deutsche Werkbund?
That may have had an influence. Gropius was one of the leading people in the Deutsche Werkbund, particularly so, say, after 1910. There was this Deutsche Werkbund exhibition in Cologne where he built one of the important buildings.[5] I think his building and Henry

van de Velde's theater were the real buildings there. He certainly was very active in the Deutsche Werkbund. There were other people, not often architects, but craftsmen. They tried to use good materials. They had a sense of quality. I had nothing to do with the Deutsche Werkbund then. I came much later. It was in 1926 when I came to the Deutsche Werkbund, when they gave me this job to do, the Weissenhofsiedlung exhibition in Stuttgart.

Has working in America changed what you think or what you do?
I think you are always influenced by your environment. There's no doubt. I think that teaching helped me a lot. I was forced to be clear to the students. Students are funny people. They perforate you with questions. You look like a sieve. You have to make it really clear and you cannot fool them. They want to know, and you have to be clear. That forced me to think those things through so that I could answer them. I think teaching had this influence. It was in the direction I was going anyway.

So that was not a waste of time as far as you were concerned?
Oh, no, no, on the opposite, I think it was really good. I don't think you have to build a thousand houses or a thousand buildings. That's all nonsense. I can make a statement about architecture with a few buildings. If I would do nothing else, that would make absolutely clear what I mean.

I remember the greatest impression I had the first time in New York: that an elevator could take you up in no time, fifty stories high, and really hit it on the head. I was very much impressed by that.

Model of the Weissenhofsiedlung, Stuttgart, Germany, 1927

You once mentioned the Pennsylvania barn.

Yes, the good Pennsylvania barn, I really like better than most buildings. It's a real building and the best building for that reason I know in America.

The Washington Bridge, I think, is a fine sample of modern building. It's directly to the point. Maybe they had ideas about these towers, but I'm talking about a principle and not about that. But to go in this simple straight line from one bank of the Hudson to the other, this direct solution, that is what I am driving at.

There's something else. We use in German the word *Baukunst*; that are two words—*Bau* (building) and *Kunst* (art). The art is the refinement of the building. That is what we express with *Baukunst*. When I was young, we hated the German word for architecture: *Architektur*. We talked about *Baukunst*, because architecture is that you form something from the outside.

Would you say that a characteristic of *Baukunst* has always been a certain reasonableness?

Yes, at least that is what I like in *Baukunst*. Even though we had to make a lot of Baroque things when I was young, I was never much interested in Baroque architecture. I was interested in structural architecture, I was interested in Romanesque, I was interested in Gothic architecture. They are often misunderstood. The profiles of a pillar in a cathedral, that is still a very clear structure. The refinements were to make it clearer, not to decorate it, but to make it clearer. People think, when they see one of these build-ings, they say it is too cold. But they forget what they are asking for, because, they think, that is too strong an order. They have it on Michigan Avenue, on the lakefront, everywhere. That is what they really ask for. They are not clear about it. They ask for chaos. But there can be a richness. It doesn't have to be chaos. I think you can use clear elements and make it rich. Any medieval city used the same plan all over. What was the difference was the doorknob or bay window and that depended on the money they had. But the plan was about all the same. They had the stable culture.

1964 What about technical developments?

People are surprised that I used construction in different materials, but that to me is absolutely normal. In the one case the roof plate is a real plate and has to be supported. It doesn't matter if you build it in steel or in concrete. Nearly all the cathedrals have the same structural principle. What is wrong with that? You can change. You need not copy it really, but you can use it as a structural principle.

That was, in fact, our idea when we started to work. We wanted to develop new structural solutions which could be used by anybody. We were not after individual solutions. We were after good structural solutions. We are not hurt if somebody uses that. We are hurt if the somebody doesn't use them well. There are certainly many more unknown students of mine than direct students. But certainly I am not hurt at all. On the opposite, that is what we tried to achieve, and we did it. There is no doubt about that.

And your sketches for the glass skyscraper?

That was another problem. There I was interested in glass and what can be done with glass buildings. I tried to avoid certain glare or dead front. So first I bent these large pieces so that they had the character of a crystal. Under no circumstances was it a dead solution. Then later I thought that maybe it could be much richer

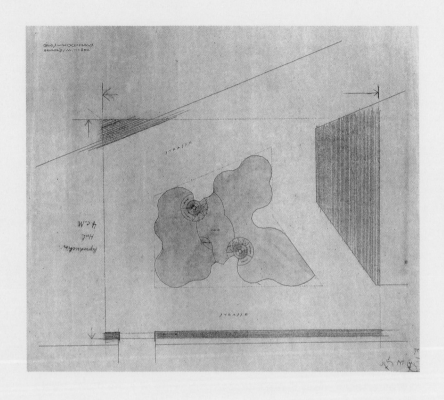

Glass skyscraper, plan and elevation, 1922

if I would make it fully curved, but they were just studies in glass. I was thinking about a building all right, but that was a particular study in glass.

As far as the buildings you now build, are they more characteristic of steel or of glass?

Some people say the Seagram Building is a bronze building. They don't talk about a glass building because there is so much metal there. I think that they are glass buildings, but that is when one works the problem through.

When you use concrete you waive the plasticity of concrete?

The plasticity of concrete, that is very funny. The plasticity of concrete is not necessarily the best way to use concrete. I think I use concrete, if I use it, in a structural manner. What I call a structure. I know you can use it in another way, but I don't like the other way. I still like it for building a clear structure. I don't care about the plastic solutions. I just don't.

Even in your chairs?

See, that is the same. The chair is an arc chair with this half circle in front of it. That is a skeleton structure. Even the Barcelona chair is still a skeleton structure. I made some designs of plastic chairs. I didn't follow them. There I used the mass. If you want to use a plastic material, then you have to use the mass. But because you can form the concrete, it is not necessary to form it in a plastic manner. It's just because that is a possibility you can do it.

You see, when we used aluminum, there you can use extruded materials. When we used it for the first time we tried it for our mullions. Then we hung it on the roof of 860–880 Lake Shore

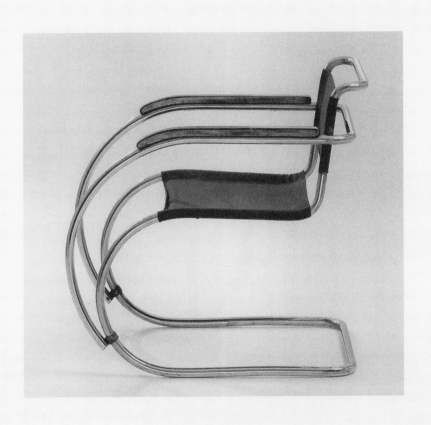

MR534 cantilevered arm chair, 1927

Drive to see how it reads. I tell you that the simple I beam worked much better. That is why we used, even in aluminum, the I beam structure. It reads better. It is much clearer.

You say clear. Do you think there's a relationship between clarity and goodness?
Yes, to me, certainly. Yes, I'm quite sure about that.

If you had lived in another period might you have used...
Oh, certainly, if we didn't have other materials; but we have steel. I think that this is a fine material. By fine, I mean it is very strong. It is very elegant. You can do a lot with it. The whole character of the building is very light. That is why I like it when I have to build a building in a steel construction. What I like best is when I can use stone on the ground and then come up a little.

Do you like steel because of the factor of economy?
It is an economy factor, but it is not an architectural factor. It is a factor here in the United States. When you have to build something, you take a sheet of paper and write down what the site costs, the architect's fee, the engineering fee, and God knows what we get back. If that is not 12 percent or 15 percent, it will never be built. That is the economical question you were talking about. Not even the greatest idea will be built if it is not economical in this sense. I am not talking about this economy. I am talking about a spiritual economy, the economy of means. The clearest sentence is, to me, economy. That is the economy that has an influence on architecture.

You can build in concrete. There are the Robert Maillart bridges in Switzerland that are wonderful bridges, very clear. I have nothing against that. But if you build in steel, it gives you a lot of freedom inside. People say, "Ah, that is cold." That's nonsense. Inside you can really do what you like. You are free to do something. But you are not free outside.

You have to remember in an enclosed building you have a few floor-plan possibilities. When you really work in one of our buildings, you will come to the conclusion there are only a few good solutions. They are limited even though you could do anything you like.

However, if the use of the building changed, say the museum building became for some reason a century from now...

Yes, it could be something else. I would not hesitate to make a cathedral in the inside of my convention hall.[6] I see no reason why not. You can do that. So a type, like the convention hall or like the museum, can be used for other purposes just as well. This is not anymore that the form follows function or should follow function. I am, anyway, a little dubious about these statements. There was a reason when somebody said it. But you cannot make a law out of them. You very well could make an apartment building from an office building. They are similar in the fact that you have twenty or thirty floors one on top of the other. That is the character of the building, not to talk about what is inside. In an apartment building you may use, for economical reasons, smaller spans or something, reduce the size, but you could very well live in an office building with the large span and have a fine apartment in that.

The sociologists tell us we have to think about the human beings who are living in that building. That is a sociological problem, not an architectural one. That always comes up. But that is a sociological question. I think the sociologists should fight that out. That is not an architectural question.

And it can't be solved architecturally?

No. It could be solved if they would give us a program. But first they have to prove that their idea is a sound one in the socio-logical field. They would like to make us responsible for that! No, not with me!

When I look at these projects I am struck by the fact that there is a sense of continuity in your work. Is there a relationship?

It is always the same problem. It is only that in one case you have just, say, walls to work with and, in this group of buildings, you have buildings to work with. But it is the same problem. You find a good relation among them. It's always the same. It is a very simple problem. We had in our school a space problem which every student had to go through and work on, and that is the same for a small apartment as it is for a hotel or a bank lobby. There is no difference in these. It is the same problem.

Is it the same for a city plan, almost?

I would say yes. In city planning you have the traffic problems, but in itself it is the same problem. It is a very simple problem of the good relation of one to another. In some we had first a free plan and then we were bound by streets, so it became a geometric plan, not a free plan. But you can make a free composition or a geometrical composition just as well. In principle there is no difference in it.

But the fact that streets are a gridiron, does this tend to suggest a . . .

Certainly, to me it suggested a geometrical solution. Not that I am for it out of principle, but that is what I have to work with. That

German Pavilion, Barcelona International Exhibition, Spain, 1929

is a material to me. I can make a building or a group of buildings. I can make it symmetrical or I can make it asymmetrical, that is just what the problem is about. Some people think it has to be asymmetrical: that is not the case. Maybe they are tired of a lot of things, and they just try something else.

I remember when I made the symmetrical solution somewhere, and I was told, now we have to learn again that there can be symmetry. But the symmetry was the reasonable solution, not that I particularly liked it or didn't like it. That was the reasonable solution for this purpose. I would not hesitate to do that. I think that is more an aesthetic speculation. I don't care much about these things.

In regard to your buildings, the Friedrich Krupp administration building, for instance...

The Krupp is an enormous skeleton building. If you use a skeleton you would come to a similar solution. You can do something that is not similar but of form is the same. The skeleton is just a skeleton.

The Science Building for Duquesne University is a laboratory.[7] Since we did not know what would be inside, we thought we would let the pipes go wherever they like to go. We made the first lab building in Chicago, the Minerals and Metals Research Building, that was kind of a laboratory, but it was not a chemical laboratory. There we used glass on the outside.

Model of the Friedrich Krupp administration building, Essen, Germany, 1961
© Hedrich-Blessing/Chicago Historical Society

Do the plans for Montreal, Toronto, and the Chicago Federal Center
have something in common?

We put the buildings so that each one gets the best situation and
that the space between them is about the best we can achieve.
They all have that in common. Even if I would build a group of
single houses, I would use the same principle there. Only that
the space between them maybe would be smaller.

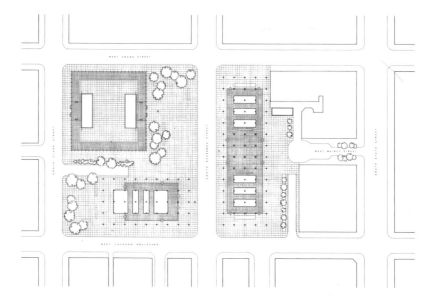

Federal Center, Chicago, 1959–73

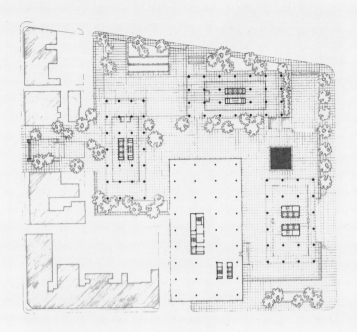

Westmount Square, Montreal, Canada, 1964–67

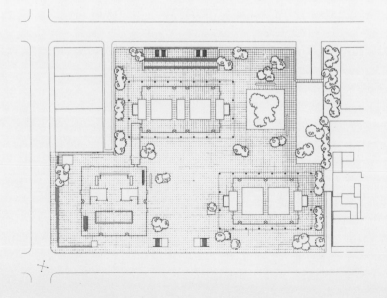

Toronto-Dominion, Toronto, Canada, 1963–69

1955 You once told me how the Barcelona Pavilion evolved around a slab of marble that you found.

We had very little time. It was deep in the winter. You cannot move marble from the quarry in the winter because it is still wet inside and it would freeze to pieces. You had to find a piece of material which is dry. We had to go and look around in huge depots. There I found an onyx block. This block had a certain size so I had only the possibility of taking twice the height of the block. Then making the pavilion twice the height of the onyx block. That was the module.

Would you be interested in doing another exhibition type of building?

I went through a lot of different possible types of building. There are only a few left. I would like to do the Convention Hall in Chicago. This is an enormous building, 722 by 620 feet. I would like to see it myself. I know the drawings. I know the idea behind it. But, in fact, there is a certain size that is a reality. Take the pyramids in Egypt and make them only 15 feet high. It is nothing. There is just this enormous size that makes all the difference.

Do you feel in the Seagram Building on Park Avenue that the size of the sheer wall going up will have a lot to do with its impact?

Yes, I am quite sure. Because of its simplicity, again, it will be much stronger. Some other buildings are much higher and richer in the grouping and so on. I think, at least that is what I hope, that the Seagram Building will be a good building.

I must say that when I came first to the United States, I lived at the New York University Club. I saw the main tower of the Rockefeller Center every morning from my breakfast table and it

Left: Seagram Building, Park Avenue, New York, 1958–60, Ezra Stoller © Esto

made a great impression on me. That slab, yes. It has nothing to do
with style. There you see that it is a mass. That is not an individual
thing, thousands of windows. Good or bad, that doesn't mean
anything. It is like an army of soldiers or like a meadow. You don't
see the details anymore when you see the mass. I think that is the
quality of this tower.

You set the Seagram Building back at a time when nobody else set
buildings back.

I set it back so that you could see it. That was the reason. If you
go to New York, you really have to look at these canopies to find
where you are. You cannot even see the building. You see only the
building in the distance. So I set it back for this reason.

Why was the material bronze?

We used bronze because of the client. Just in the talk we had,
he said, "I like bronze and marble." I said, "That's good enough
for me!"

In designing your building the way you do, somehow the Seagram
respects other buildings like the McKim, Mead, and White building
across the street.

Oh, certainly, yes. The Lever House was there when we started.[8]
When we moved the building back, we didn't know what would
happen on each side of it. After the Seagram Building was
finished, there you had the Lever House and the Seagram Building,
so it was quite easy to set back the next building that is right
between them. But they didn't! That was so funny. That was a
great help for any architect, but that is just what happens.

Previous pages: Convention Hall, Chicago, 1953–54

Unlike the Seagram Building, the two Bacardi buildings[8] posed different problems.

Yes, it was certainly a different site. In the first building in Santiago de Cuba, the client wanted to have a large room. That is what he liked. He said, "I like to have a desk in a large room. I like to work with my people. I don't need a closed office because I work more than anybody else, so it doesn't hurt me that they see me." We tried to solve that.

But in Mexico there were two factors which changed the character of the building. The one was that the highway is higher than the site. So if we would have built a one-story building there, you would see only the roof. That was the reason why we made a two-story building there. It was a more normal office building because the leading people insisted on separate offices.

How important do you regard historical influences?

I am not interested in the history of civilization. I am interested in our civilization. We are living it. Because I really believe, after a long time of working and thinking and studying, that architecture has, in fact, only to do with this civilization we are in. That is really what architecture is about. It can only express this civilization we are in and nothing else. There are certain forces that are in contrast to each other. But if you really look at it, you'll find leading forces, sustaining forces, and you'll find superficial forces. That is why it is so difficult to give a definition of civilization and to give a definition of our time. In older civilizations the superficial forces are gone. Only the deciding forces become historical forces, the exceptional forces.

Often you cannot make a definition of something. But then you see something that strikes you in the bones. That is it. You cannot express it, but that is it. It's like when you meet somebody who is healthy. What could you say, but you know when somebody is healthy or not. That is what I find so important, particularly in the time we are in now when this Baroque movement is going on. You call it Baroque or whatever. But I think it is a form of Baroque movement against the reasonable, the direct. In particular, in the time where there is confusion, what could be leading if not reason? That is why we were trying so hard since the 1920s, the early 1920s, to find what is a reasonable way to do things. There were people who had a lot of fantasy and sculptural interest in the Jugendstil and the Art Nouveau period. They all were, more or less, fantastic. But very few were reasonable then. I decided when I was quite young to accept this reasonableness.

1955 Do you think that new ways of living will change things?

No, I think in principle it will be the same. It can be richer as it develops. It is very difficult just to make something clear. Then express it in a beautiful way. They are two different things. But first it has to be clear. I cannot help it if somebody wants to have forty-story apartments and the apartments have to be all the same. I can only try to express it in a way that it really comes out and that in the end it is beautiful.

Are you optimistic about the future of architecture?

Certainly, I am. I am absolutely optimistic. I think you should not plan too much and not construct too much these things.

So do you envision a time later when a person working from your architectural style may evolve a richer...

I would not even use this word "style" for that. I would say if he would use the same principle, the same approach. Then he, certainly, if he is talented, he can make it richer. That depends, but it would be in principle not different.

There is obviously visible now a reaction to my approach in architecture. There is no question, but I think it is just a reaction. I don't believe it is a new approach. It is a reaction against something that is there. The reaction is a kind of fashion.

New York, 1955; Chicago, 1964

1. Mies built a house for Alois Riehl, professor in philosophy at the Friedrich Wilhelm University in Potsdam-Badelsweg (1906–7).
2. Mies was working for Peter Behrens in Berlin from 1908 to 1911.
3. Mies was director of the Bauhaus in Dessau and Berlin from 1930 to 1933.
4. Lecture at the Blackstone Hotel in Chicago, 18 May 1953: "The fact that it [the Bauhaus] was an idea, I think, is the cause of the enormous influence the Bauhaus had on any progessive school around the world. You cannot do that with organization, you cannot do that with propaganda. Only an idea spreads so far." Published in Sigfried Giedion, *Walter Gropius* (New York: Dover Publications, 1992), 18. Originally published as *Mensch und Werk* (Stuttgart: Gerd Hatje, 1954), 20–22.
5. Walter Gropius and Adolf Meyer built a factory, office building, and machinery hall for the Deutsche Werkbund exhibition in Cologne, Germany, 1914.
6. Convention Hall, Chicago, Illinois, 1953–54.
7. Science Building for Duquesne University, Pittsburgh, Pennsylvania, 1962–65.
8. Skidmore, Owings & Merrill (SOM), Lever House, New York, New York, 1950–52.
9. Bacardi headquarters, Santiago de Cuba, Cuba, 1957; Bacardi headquarters, Mexico City, Mexico, 1958–61.

Mies's American Period and Its Relevance Today
Iñaki Ábalos

It is problematic to consider the talks and interviews Mies conducted with colleagues and journalists during his American period—particularly toward its end—as "conversations." By that time Mies had already reached the conclusion that the alliance of technology and architecture would produce an architecture whose real purpose would be to express its time. In addition he believed the effort to develop a common architectural language from which a modern grammar could arise must continue. He believed this language to be already present in his work and considered it as the intermediary—the interface that really spoke to people and expressed itself and its time. The reader thus encounters a Mies who is laconic and stubborn, who uses the language of someone who believes he has achieved maturity in his style, and has reached a stage where no questions or incentives remain except to complete the scope of his style in terms of technique, scale, materials, and typology. Mies is bringing his artistic autobiography to a close, as it were. But it becomes evident from this collection of conversations that he saw—with some apprehension—a world around him that seemed to be moving in another direction, starting to escape his grasp. This was a world connected to his professional life, so he thought he understood it well and had the authority to warn against the more banal deviations.

In particular, we see a Mies who is worried about the fluid forms that began to emerge during that period and who is wary of criticism of the monotony and tedium into which his "common language" and "rationality" could degenerate when disseminated. He keeps referring to his early years when talking about this, emphasizing the word "fantasy" and warning against extreme subjectivity, which, in his view, should only be permissible for painters, since rationality is inherent to the very notion of architecture. He believes that the right way to achieve monumentality—an idea of modern beauty in built form—is through the common language, and he makes a corresponding effort to transmit his vision.

In his American phase Mies set about reducing the range of architecture to three models or types, defined mainly by their dimensions and the resulting structural problems: one-story or two-story pavilions, usually quite small or medium-sized; large, translucent halls that are developed horizontally; and vertical buildings or skyscrapers, which in his mind comprise all structures with floors piled on top of each other.

The pavilions—from the Farnsworth House to Crown Hall at the Illinois Institute of Technology (IIT)—strove for a good relationship with the ground-floor level, for a slight dominance (to "see and be seen") and the greatest clarity in defining a canonic modern house.

Mies considered the large hall a place for the collective—the public—so for him it had monumental character. It could be a factory (Bacardi), a museum (Berlin), or a convention center (which he claimed could in turn be transformed into a cathedral). His thinking in these cases does not vary, since the problem is as much structural as monumental: sometimes the size dictates a complicated structural approach in order to achieve an efficiency that corresponds to the development of technology. He also believes that the common language—at a certain scale and when representing something for society—only works if it follows the language of monuments, of "great form"—a term he uses when discussing Peter Behrens.

The third type, the skyscraper, marked Mies's American career. With his skyscraper designs he began to develop a real artistic biography, and they were also the link between his youth and maturity. As a practical task that is repetitive, systematic, and requires order and clarity, the skyscraper was one of his favorite themes.

For Mies, the skyscraper was the organism in which modernity combined all its energy, organizational capacity, and rationality, and he knew that only his work, with its abstinence from decoration—and precisely because of this abstinence—could achieve the coherent form that is the best expression of the modern style. As with the large hall, the common language is again the gateway to monumental language. The skyscraper has become a modern monument because for twenty years Mies sustained the idea that its function and scale do not matter: housing or offices look the same; it does not matter whether the building is twenty or forty stories high—the first floor is the same as the top floor—according to the pure technical logic that led to Mies's aesthetic canon.

Mies was conscious of his authority. Having defined the modern skyscraper and then built it, he saw how his ideas extended to large office blocks of the SOM type and appeared in the same vein in all American and European cities. These buildings create a universal chorus that, in turn, confirms the legitimacy and scope of Mies's common language, while at the same time erecting bars around this language—a cage of corporate and bureaucratic connotations—which initiated criticism of his work. Mies, however, had no problems with this bureaucratic character, because it is essentially what the skyscraper embodies: the bureaucracy of modern society in material form. He understood that these criticisms were based on a passing fashion, and time has confirmed his belief.

His acquired wisdom enabled Mies to discourse with his interviewers at a level that hardly touches them: he did not talk with them; there was no complicity, surprise, or interaction—none of the elements that make a conversation a productive activity. Mies set

94

up a particular dialog: not with his time and what he represents, but with other moments, other times—with architecture and history. "That's good enough for me!," he said when his clients proposed to build the Seagram Building out of bronze and marble, and used these materials as the load-bearing structure and ribbing of a curtain wall that literally reproduced what he had tried in steel and glass. Thus Mies provided the key to understanding the relationship between the common language and overall form, and between technology and monument. His manifesto "Architecture and Technology" (see pages 8–9) shows the scope of his position: "Our real hope is that they grow together [architecture and technology], that someday the one be the expression of the other. Only then will we have an architecture worthy of its name: Architecture as a true symbol of our time." This is the vision of someone who represents this position—and who believes in his heart of hearts that he has already reached that goal—and he talks about it using repetitive sentences that reflect some indifference toward his contemporaries.

More than fifty years have passed, and we see his words in another context. For a different generation this search for accord between technology and architecture—and for a common language—has been eliminated, swept away by a boom of the spectacular and original, of differentiation, the unusual, and the biographical. This might suggest that this document's only value is as a testimonial that is rather opaque in relation to the present and has merely historical interest. But my impression is different. In the 1970s we attended Mies's postmodern funeral: Leon Krier's drawings, which caricatured Miesian interiors using Nazi symbols, and Stanley Tigerman's collage of Crown Hall sinking like the *Titanic* in the seething waters of postmodernism. But the sight of those hurried funerals was pathetic. Nobody remembers those individuals today, and in the 1990s unprecedented interest in Mies took the form of a great variety of books, catalogs, and exhibitions on him, which were rich and of a high intellectual standard. Even Le Corbusier's previously unchallenged authority as the leading star of modernism was thrown into crisis. People want to revisit Mies in his many aspects, and I predict that the contrast of his work with the "playground for children" (in Mies's words, see page 9) will mature in due course, although the latter is favored in commercial circles, because the spectacular and surprising are so valuable for marketing. My prediction is not so much the result of a writer's improbable power of prophecy, but stems from a recent perception that the most advanced pedagogy has changed direction. Recent teaching looks indulgently at the formal and digital passion oi the "vanguardist" direction—promoted by Bernard Tschumi at Columbia University at the beginning of the 1990s—as if it were a naive era. Today the value of discipline is reintroduced by revising the relationship between technology and architecture. This development takes place in the context of evolving digital technologies and takes a pragmatic approach, reconsidering the "plan" as the only efficient future instrument of control and using digitization to bring together design and production.

During these past fifty years there have been clear changes—in technology, society, architecture, and the cultural role of architecture. However, the American Mies fascinates those who dare to take a step back and who hope to generate a discussion that will bring in some control over the blind, chaotic, and hyperactive present. And what they achieve on a personal level, Mies's works achieve with the same authority in the professional sphere. The Seagram Building still demonstrates this, exercising its authority and control over an immense part of Manhattan. It is not the highest, most eccentric, or the boldest skyscraper. Simply, it is the most perfect.

Illustration Credits